ADVENTURES WITH ROCKS AND MINERALS

GEOLOGY EXPERIMENTS FOR YOUNG PEOPLE

Lloyd H. Barrow

ENSLOW PUBLISHERS, INC.

Bloy St. & Ramsey Ave.	P.O. Box 38
Box 777	Aldershot
Hillside, N.J. 07205	Hants GU12 6BP
U.S.A.	U.K.

DEDICATION

To my father Robert and late mother Pearl who encouraged me to always try new adventures— this is my first book.

ACKNOWLEDGMENT

I wish to thank Sandy Burr for her editorial assistance; Katherine Nelms, Patricia Kennedy, and Lynn Coffey for typing; members of my family, Rosemary, Lon, and Valerie, for their support and encouragement; and fellow teachers for their comments and suggestions during the preparation of this book.

Library of Congress Cataloging-in-Publication Data

Barrow, Lloyd H.
    Adventures with rocks and minerals: geology experiments for young people / Lloyd H. Barrow
        p. cm.
    Summary: Uses earth science experiments for home or school to demonstrate the properties of rocks and minerals and how they relate to important environmental concerns such as earthquakes, erosion, acid rain, and water pollution.
    ISBN 0-89490-263-6
    1. Earth sciences—Experiments—Juvenile literature. [1. Rocks—Experiments. 2. Mineralogy—Experiments. 3. Earth sciences—Experiments. 4. Experiments.] I. Title
QE44.837   1991
550.87—dc20   90-30444
                                                    CIP
                                                    AC

Printed in the United States of America
10 9 8 7 6 5 4 3

Illustrated by Kimberly Austin

CONTENTS

INTRODUCTION

GEOLOGY

Right under our feet the earth is changing. Rocks are forming from molten materials deep down in the center of the earth. Continents are moving. Mountains are rising and then slowly wearing away.

People who study the earth and how it changes are called geologists. They learn about the earth by making observations and by asking questions and then by experimenting to find the answers. Some of the questions geologists ask are easy to answer. To find out if a diamond can scratch glass, a geologist just gets a diamond and some glass and observes what happens when the diamond is rubbed against the glass. But some of the questions are trickier, such as, "How old is the earth?" and "How do mountains form?" As geologists find answers to their questions, they always come up with new questions and experiments. This book is a collection of experiments that you can do at home or in school. Doing them will help you learn how to ask questions and find answers and how to become a better observer. No one will ever know everything about geology—but it's great fun to learn as much as you can about it.

THE EARTH

Geologists believe that the earth is over four-and-a-half billion years old. When it first formed, it was so hot that it was molten—liquid rock. Over the ages the outside layer of the earth, called the crust, has slowly turned solid, but most of the inside is still molten. As continents form and move over millions of years, pressures deep inside the earth cause earthquakes and volcanoes. As layers of rock push against one another, moved by these forces inside the earth, sometimes they fold over one another the way a stack of washcloths folds up if you push on both ends. This folding is one of the ways mountains form. Another way mountains form is when the pressure inside the earth splits a layer of rock. The split is called a fault. Once mountains form, wind and rain slowly wear them away in a process called weathering. In caves, crystal structures called stalactites and stalagmites are slowly forming. These changes take place over thousands, or even millions, of years, and so people can't observe them firsthand. But geologists can observe how things are today and read about how things were a hundred years ago from earlier scientists who wrote down their observations. Then they can make educated guesses (hypotheses) about how things came to be this way and how they might change in the future. Geologists can never be absolutely certain that their hypotheses are right, but experiments help them to learn if they are probably on the right track.

Rocks are made up of minerals—crystals of different chemicals. Each mineral has its own special properties. In order to identify a mineral, geologists observe its color and shape and experiment to discover its other properties.

Geologists classify rocks into three types, based on the three ways that rocks form. (1) Igneous rocks form from molten rock that hardens as it cools down. Lava from volcanoes turns into igneous rock. (2) As rocks are worn away by moving water or wind, they are sometimes ground into sand or silt. Sedimentary rock forms when this sand or silt is pressed and cemented together. Sandstone is an example of sedimentary rock. (3) If an igneous or sedimentary rock is heated and compressed by forces in the earth so much that its minerals are changed, it forms a metamorphic rock. Marble is a metamorphic rock.

Soil is formed by the breaking down of rocks by weathering and the actions of living things. This process takes such a long time that when soil is carried away by the wind or rain, which is called erosion, it may not be replaced for thousands of years. Consequently, soil is very valuable, which is why geologists study it and help farmers to conserve it.

Geologists also study earthquakes. The more they learn about them from the past, and the more observations they make about the present earthquakes, the better they can warn us about future ones. They measure how strong an earthquake is on a machine called a seismograph. The machine describes the force of the earthquake with a number from 1 to 10 on what is called the Richter scale.

Acid rain is another area of concern for geologists. Acid chemicals that are sent up into the air from car exhausts and industry smoke-stacks return to earth in rain and snow. Acid rain damages buildings and statues, pollutes lakes, streams, and the ocean, and poisons trees and other plants. Geologists study acid rain to learn how acidic it is and what its effects on the earth are.

ADVENTURES WITH GEOLOGY

This book is a collection of questions and experiments to help you understand how a geologist studies the earth. Each experiment has five parts. The <u>materials</u> part lists what you need. The <u>procedure</u> explains how to do the experiment safely. The <u>observations</u> suggest some of the things to look for. The <u>discussion</u> explains what your observations may tell you about geology. The <u>other things to try</u> part suggest more questions and gives you hints about how to find out more about geology.

SAFETY NOTE

WHEN YOU DO THESE EXPERIMENTS MAKE SURE YOU
1. Get an adult's permission before using anything in your home.
2. Ask an adult to watch you do the experiment. Grownups are interested in the earth, too!
3. Carefully follow the directions for each experiment.
4. Clean up when you're finished.
5. Have fun!

WHAT ARE THE COLOR PROPERTIES OF MINERALS?

Materials

Hand lens or magnifying glass

Mineral samples such as calcite, galena, gypsum, halite, hematite, magnetite, pyrite, quartz, talc, etc. (available at rock shops)

Unglazed porcelain tile (back of a ceramic tile) or streak plate

Paper

Procedure

Examine each sample with your hand lens and record the name and color of each mineral on your paper. Examine each mineral to see whether or not it reflects light. When it reflects light, this property is called luster. If a mineral reflects light like a metal or shiny surface, then it is described as having a metallic luster. When a mineral doesn't reflect much light, then it is described as having a nonmetallic luster. Record the luster of each mineral. Scratch each mineral on the piece of unglazed porcelain tile. This mineral residue is called streak. Using your hand lens, examine the streak color of the mineral left on the tile. Record the streak color of each mineral.

Observations

Do all minerals reflect light the same way? Is luster or color better to use to identify minerals? Do all minerals leave a streak? What is the typical streak color for nonmetallic luster minerals? Which minerals are easy to identify from their streak color? Which minerals are hard to identify from their streak color?

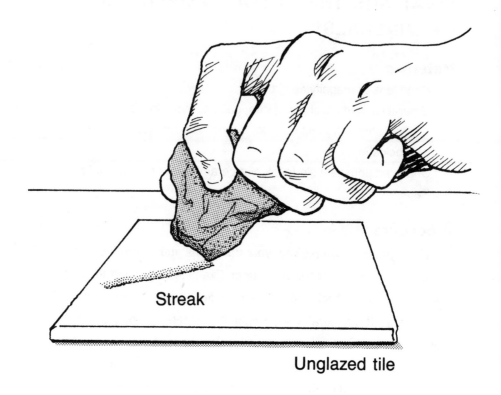

Streak

Unglazed tile

Discussion

The color of a mineral is one of its properties. But some minerals can have more than one color. For example, quartz can be either clear (colorless), purple, rose (pink), or milky, but its streak color will always be white or colorless. Therefore, geologists will use mainly the streak color and type of luster rather than the overall color of the mineral to identify it.

The porcelain tile (streak plate) is harder than the mineral; therefore, when the mineral is rubbed, a fine powder is left on the porcelain. Usually nonmetallic minerals leave a streak that is colorless or very lightly colored. Metallic minerals usually leave a dark streak. Some minerals are too hard to leave a powder residue, so the streak test doesn't always work.

Other things to try

Determine how the luster changes when minerals are left outside for two weeks.

Determine how the metallic luster of a mineral changes when left in a glass of water for a week.

HOW HARD ARE MINERALS?

2

Materials

Nail file (metal)   Pennies
Glass plate or baby-food jar   Chart paper
Mineral samples such as calcite, galena, gypsum, halite,
    hematite, magnetite, pyrite, quartz, talc, etc. (available at
    rock shops)

Procedure

Rub the nail file once across a penny. The scratch on the penny tells you that the nail file is harder than the penny. Rub the nail file and the penny on your fingernail and on a glass plate. Use the scratch test to find out the <u>hardness</u> of each of these items. Using the following hardness scale, discover how hard or soft each mineral is:

Very soft—scratched with a fingernail

Soft—penny will scratch it but a fingernail will not

Medium—will scratch the glass

Hard—will scratch the nail file

Record the results on your chart paper, arranging each mineral in order from hardest to softest.

Observations

Which mineral was the softest? Which mineral was the hardest? Do any minerals have the same hardness? Which ones? Which mineral has the same hardness as a penny? As glass? What would explain why all minerals do not leave a streak?

Discussion

A specific mineral always has the same hardness even if it comes in different colors. A mineral that can scratch another mineral is the

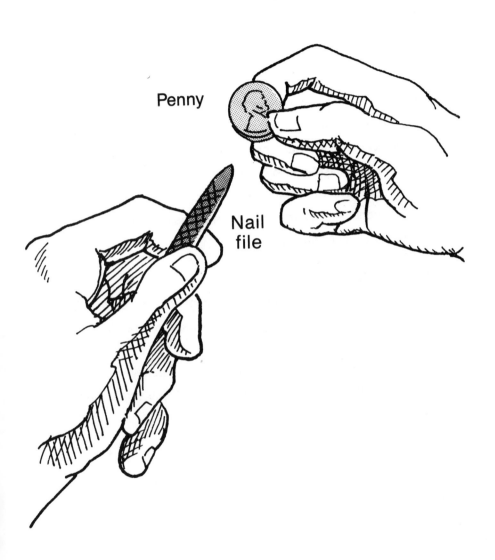

Penny

Nail
file

harder of the two. Mohs' scale, which geologists use, is a scale of the hardness of minerals. The scale ranks hardness between the numbers 1 and 10. The harder the mineral, the higher the number on the Mohs' scale. The softest mineral is talc. It measures 1 on the scale. The hardest mineral is diamond. It measures 10 on the scale. If you don't have a Moh's hardness kit, you can use other things that geologists have discovered to test hardness. Your fingernail has a hardness of 2, the penny is 3, the glass plate is 5.5, and the nail file is 6.5. Different minerals can have the same streak color, but they probably have different hardnesses. By knowing the hardness of a mineral, you can be more certain of its name.

Other things to try

Test other minerals and rank them in order from hardest to softest. How do your results from this test compare with earlier tested minerals?

Are all metallic luster minerals harder than a penny?

Which minerals will write on your sidewalk? (Be sure to have an adult's permission to try this experiment.)

WHAT CAUSES SOME MINERALS TO BREAK WITH FLAT SURFACES?

3

Materials

Single-edged razor blade   Small hammer

Protractor   Paper

Small flat board   Modeling clay

Hand lens or magnifying glass

Mineral samples of halite and hematite (available at rock shops)

Procedure

ASK AN ADULT TO DO THIS EXPERIMENT WHILE YOU MAKE OBSERVATIONS.

Take the piece of halite and place it flat side down in the modeling clay. Put the clay with the halite on the board. Place the sharp edge of the razor blade straight on the halite. Gently tap the razor blade with the hammer until the halite breaks. Notice the resulting flat, smooth surfaces on the halite. When a mineral splits apart with one or more flat surfaces, it has a property called <u>cleavage</u>. Using the hand lens, look for thin lines inside the halite crystal. Take the smallest piece of the halite and gently hit it with a hammer. Each of the small pieces of halite has the same cleavage. Lay the largest piece of halite on the paper and trace its outline. Using the protractor, measure the angles of each corner.

Repeat the procedure for hematite. Notice that when hematite breaks, it breaks into either rough surfaces, splintery surfaces, or smooth, curved surfaces. The surface of the hematite is rough and uneven. When a mineral breaks without a flat, smooth surface, it is called <u>fracture</u>. With this uneven breaking pattern, there is no reason to measure the angles because the angles will not always be the

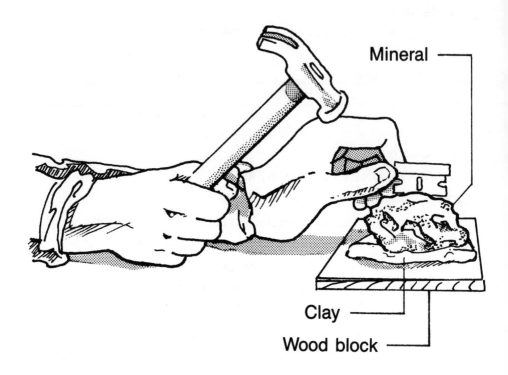

Mineral

Clay

Wood block

same. Therefore, the angles would not help us in identifying the mineral.

Observations

How many flat surfaces does halite have before and after it breaks? What was the angle of halite's corners? What was the breaking pattern of the hematite?

Discussion

The way a mineral breaks helps us in identifying that mineral. A mineral cleaves in the area where it is the weakest. There is no relationship between hardness and cleavage. Minerals like galena and calcite always break with three different flat surfaces while halite cleaves with two different flat surfaces. The angles of halite and galena are each 90 degrees. Geologists use the number of cleavage surfaces and the angle to identify minerals.

You need to be careful when you are testing for a mineral break because such a procedure involves breaking the mineral. Since this test can destroy an entire piece, geologists try to test for other properties before they break the mineral.

Other things to try

Repeat the experiment to determine the cleavage pattern of calcite and galena.

Compare the cleavage pattern of minerals that are harder than a piece of glass and those that are softer than a piece of glass.

WHAT OTHER TESTS ARE USED TO IDENTIFY MINERALS?

4

Materials

White vinegar

Medicine dropper

Ceramic magnet

Piece of chalk

Plastic cups

Steel nails

Mineral samples such as calcite, galena, gypsum, halite, hematite, magnetite, pyrite, quartz, talc, etc. (available at rock shops)

Procedure

Part 1: Vinegar is a weak acid that is used to see if a rock has calcium carbonate. If it is present, the vinegar causes a fizz. Put a piece of chalk in a cup and add six drops of vinegar. The fizzing shows that chalk contains calcium carbonate. Put mineral samples in separate labeled cups and add six drops of vinegar to each sample. Look to see which minerals fizz. Record the minerals that fizz and those that don't. Rinse off the samples. Clean the cups.

Part 2: Touch the ceramic magnet to the steel nails. The nails are attracted to the magnet. Touch the magnet to each mineral. Record which minerals are attracted to the magnet and those that are not.

Observations

Which minerals have calcium carbonate? Which minerals are attracted to the magnet? Are there any minerals that have calcium carbonate and are attracted to the magnet?

Discussion

Geologists use the weak acid vinegar to identify all carbonate minerals and rocks (calcite, chalk, limestone, dolomite, and marble).

Chalk

The vinegar reacts when calcium carbonate is present. The more calcium carbonate present, the faster it bubbles. Carbonates can be used as a mineral supplement for people to help prevent some bone diseases. Also, some animals, like clams and oysters, have calcium carbonate in their shells.

Some minerals have special properties that geologists use to help identify them. <u>Magnetism</u> is one example. Geologists carry small magnets to locate minerals that contain iron and are mined for the iron ore. Magnetite is one and is sometimes called <u>lodestone</u>. Nails will stick to large pieces of lodestone.

Other things to try

Compare hardness with acid test results. Do all soft minerals bubble with vinegar?

What things in your room are attracted to your magnet?

HOW DO CRYSTALS GROW?

5

Materials

Colored saucer	Measuring cup
Rock salt	String, unwashed
Teaspoon	Pint Mason jar
Coffee filter	Small saucepan
Pencil	Washer
Rubberband	Water
Hand lens or magnifying glass	

Procedure

ASK AN ADULT TO HELP YOU WITH THIS EXPERIMENT. DO NOT USE THE STOVE BY YOURSELF.

Heat 1/2 cup (about 125 ml) of water in a small saucepan until the water boils. Turn off the heat. Slowly stir into the hot water as much rock salt, about 1 cup (about 250 ml), as will dissolve. Continue stirring until all the salt is dissolved (about one minute). Let the salt water cool for thirty minutes. Pour four teaspoons into a colored saucer and set the saucer aside.

Put a coffee filter across the top of a Mason jar. Fold one-third of the coffee filter over the edge of the jar and secure with a rubberband. Pour the remaining salt water slowly through the filter. Leave the jar alone for twenty-four hours. The next day, check to see if crystals are left in the bottom of the jar and/or on the coffee filter. Use the hand lens to study the crystals. Compare these crystals with those on the colored saucer. Remove the coffee filter and dispose of it in whatever place an adult directs you.

On the second day, cut a piece of string three inches (about 8 cm) longer than the height of the jar. Tie the pencil to one end of the string and the washer to the other end. Rub some salt onto the string and

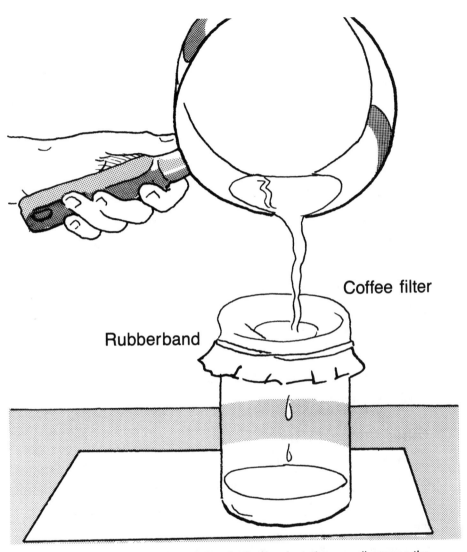

Rubberband

Coffee filter

place the string with the washer in the jar. Lay the pencil across the top of the jar. Do not move the jar for several days. Check daily for crystals without removing the string.

Observations

What do the salt crystals on the saucer and string look like? Are they all the same size and shape? What did you find on the coffee filter? How long did it take before you could see crystals on the string? What happens to the size and shape of the crystals as they grow? Where are the most crystals found: on the string, the bottom of the jar, or the sides of the jar?

Discussion

The salt water has a lot of dissolved salt. As the water evaporates, the dissolved salt sticks to the string. Rubbing salt on the string provides a starting place for the salt crystals to grow. It takes longer when you don't rub the string.

When salt water cools fast, the crystals will be small. Slow cooling gives more time for larger crystals. When you find a rock with large crystals, it was probably formed inside the earth and cooled slowly. Rocks with small crystals were cooled at the surface. The shape and size of crystals helps us identify different minerals and the area in which they were formed.

Other things to try

Repeat the experiment using alum, borax, or colored sugar. How do these crystals' shapes and sizes compare with salt crystals?

Repeat the experiment, adding several drops of food coloring to the boiling salt water.

Repeat the salt experiment, putting half of the salt water in the refrigerator for fast cooling and keeping the other half at room temperature. After twenty-four hours, compare the size of the salt crystals.

HOW DOES THE COOLING RATE AFFECT CRYSTAL SIZE?

6

Materials

Measuring cup

Rock salt

Teaspoon

Coffee filter

Two pencils

Rubberband

Refrigerator

Hand lens or magnifying glass

String, unwashed

Two pint Mason jars

Small saucepan

Two washers

Water

Procedure

ASK AN ADULT TO HELP YOU WITH THIS EXPERIMENT. DO NOT USE THE STOVE BY YOURSELF.

Heat 1 cup (about 250 ml) of water in a small saucepan until the water boils. Turn off the heat. Slowly stir into the hot water as much rock salt, about 1 cup (about 250 ml), as will dissolve. Continue stirring until all the salt is dissolved (about one minute). Let the salt water cool for thirty minutes. Put a coffee filter across the top of each of the two Mason jars. Fold one-third of the coffee filter over the edge of each jar and secure with a rubberband. Pour half of the salt water into a measuring cup. Then pour it slowly through each filter. Remove the coffee filter and dispose of it wherever an adult tells you. Place one jar in the refrigerator, and leave the other jar on the counter. Leave the jars alone for twenty-four hours. The next day, check to see if crystals are left in the bottom of each jar. Use the hand lens to study the crystals.

On the second day, cut two pieces of string three inches (about 8 cm) longer than the height of each jar. Tie one end of each piece of the string around a pencil and the other ends around a washer. Laying

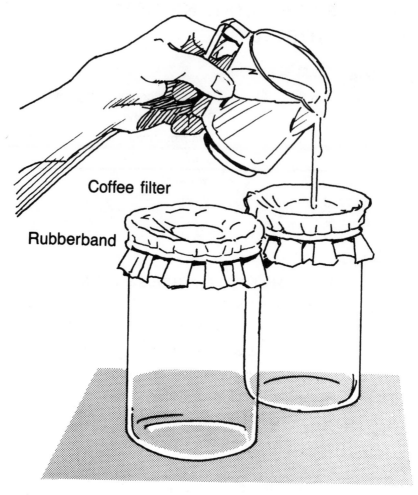

Coffee filter

Rubberband

the pencils across the jars will prevent the string from falling into the jars. Rub some salt onto the two pieces of string before putting them into separate jars. Place the strings with the washers in the jars. Do not move the jars for several days. Check daily for crystals without removing the string.

Observations

What do the salt crystals in the jar in the refrigerator and in the jar on the counter look like? Are they all the same size and shape? How long did it take before you could see crystals on the string? What happens to the size and shape of the crystals as they grow? Would crystals that are cooling inside the earth be larger or smaller than those cooling on the outside of the earth?

Discussion

The salt water has a lot of dissolved salt. As the water evaporates, the dissolved salt sticks to the string. Rubbing salt on the string provides a starting place for the salt crystals to grow. Crystals grow more slowly when you don't rub salt on the string.

When salt water cools quickly, the crystals don't have much time to grow. They tend to be small in size. Slow cooling allows the crystals more time to grow, and they are consequently larger in size. When hot lava comes from a volcano and the lava cools outside the earth, the crystals are small. But when the lava stays inside the earth, the temperature cools more slowly. These crystals will be larger. When you find a rock with large crystals, it was probably formed inside the earth and cooled slowly. Rocks with small crystals were probably cooled quickly at the surface.

The jar left on the counter represents crystals that cooled inside the earth. The jar in the refrigerator represents lava from a volcano that spilled into the earth's surface.

Other things to try

Repeat the experiment, using alum, borax, or colored sugar. How do these crystals' shapes and sizes compare with the salt crystals?

Repeat the experiment, adding several drops of food coloring to the boiling salt water.

HOW MANY SIZES ARE THERE OF SAND CRYSTALS?

7

Materials

>   Two types of sandpaper (fine and coarse)
>
>   Hand lens or magnifying glass
>
>   Sandbox or beach sand
>
>   A pair of old pantyhose (foot part only)
>
>   Shoebox or any large container
>
>   Two plastic soda bottles

Procedure

Using the hand lens, examine the sand on the coarse sandpaper. Notice the size of the sand particles and the corners of the sand particles. Gently rub the sandpaper across the soda bottle. Using your hand lens, look at the scratches made on the soda bottle. Repeat, scratching the fine sandpaper on a different soda bottle.

Look at the sand from a sandbox or the beach. Compare the size, color, and shape of the sand particles. Put two handfuls of sand in the foot part of the pantyhose and gently shake over an empty shoebox.

Observations

Which type of sandpaper has the largest sand grains? Which type of sandpaper made the widest single scratch on your soda bottle? Which type of sandpaper made the most scratches on your soda bottle? How did the sand particles that stayed in the pantyhose compare with those that passed through the pantyhose? Are all the sand particles the same color? If not, what is the most common color?

Discussion

Sand is one of our most common resources. The different colors

Sandpaper

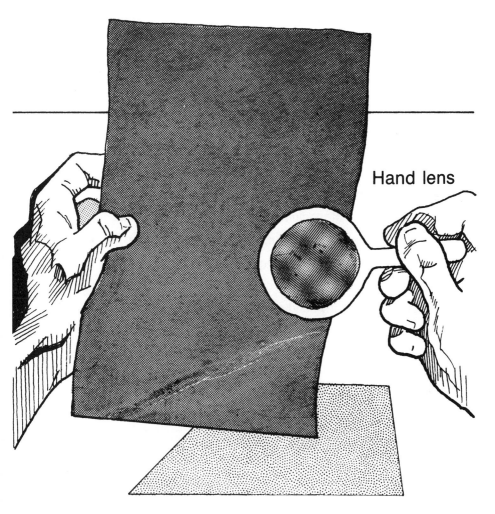

Hand lens

of sand are the result of the different minerals that make it up. The place where sand is found tells geologists about it. When the corners are smooth and shiny, the sand has been carried by water. As it is carried, the sand particles hit against each other, rubbing off the edges. When the corners are sharp, it hasn't been carried by water.

The normal pantyhose openings will let only the small sand particles through. The larger particles will stay inside the pantyhose. The pantyhose is a type of filter that sorts according to size. Filters with different-sized openings are used to sort the sand for the various kinds of sandpaper. One with a small opening is used for fine sandpaper.

Other Things to Try

Get a piece of medium sandpaper. Predict how this sandpaper will scratch a soda bottle in comparison with the other two kinds of sandpaper. Test your predictions.

Take a dime and place it on the sandpaper. Draw a circle around the dime. How many sand particles are there in a circle the size of a dime for the fine, medium, and coarse sandpaper?

HOW DOES MOVING WATER AFFECT ROCKS?

8

Materials

Two 2-liter plastic soda bottles   Measuring cup

Aquarium gravel or   Bucket

    small driveway gravel   Two clear drinking glasses

Hand lens or magnifying glass

Procedure

Gently empty the gravel into the bucket. Pour water into the bucket until it is at least 1 inch (about 2.5 cm) higher than the gravel. Gently stir with your hand until the gravel is clean. Examine the washed gravel with your hand lens. Notice the shape of the gravel, especially the corners and color of the gravel. Put 1 cup (about 250 ml) of gravel into one of the soda bottles. Add water until the bottle is one-third full. Screw the lid on tight. Shake the bottle 750 times rapidly (about five minutes). Friends can help! Immediately after shaking, pour some of the water and gravel into a clear glass. Examine the gravel with your hand lens. Notice the corners of the gravel and color of the gravel. Dump the water outside in a place recommended by an adult because it could plug the sink.

In another soda bottle, put 1 cup (about 250 ml) of gravel. Screw the lid on tight and shake 750 times rapidly. Friends can help again. Open the bottle and dump the gravel onto a flat surface. With your hand lens, examine the gravel.

Observations

What was the shape of the gravel before and after shaking in the bottle with water? What was the shape of the gravel before and after shaking in the bottle without water? How did the bottle with water affect

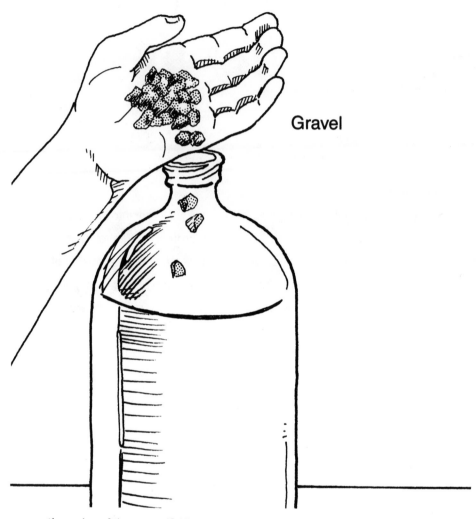

Gravel

the color of the gravel? How did the water affect the weathering of the gravel?

Discussion

Small rocks, like the gravel, are carried by rivers and streams. In the process, they bump into other rocks, and small pieces break off. The jagged edges are the first things that are broken off. Eventually, only smooth pieces of rock will be left. The breaking of the rocks into smaller pieces is called <u>weathering</u>. The next time you visit a river or a beach, you will be able to see some smooth rocks that have been weathered.

The gravel without water also was weathered when the pieces of gravel bumped into one another. When rocks fall down a hill or mountain in a rockslide, they break into smaller pieces. Strong winds are able to move very small pieces of rock and soil, and when the wind-blown particles hit something, parts of them may break off. Geologists can examine a rock and describe the amount of weathering that has taken place. However, they aren't certain whether weathering was caused by water, falling, wind, or combinations of these methods.

Some people make a hobby of polishing rocks. They put rocks in an electric tumbler that turns them similar to the way you did when you shook the soda bottle. The rocks need to be tumbled for hours. Frequently, these polished rocks are called <u>gems</u>.

Other things to try

Add 4 cups (about 1,000 ml) of water to the bottle that had no water. Pour some of the water into a clear glass. How does this compare to the bottle with gravel and water?

Repeat the experiment, shaking the bottle 250 or 500 times. Is the water as dirty? Are the pieces of gravel as smooth?

Repeat the experiment, substituting rock salt (ice-cream salt) for the gravel.

WHAT DOES FREEZING WATER DO TO ROCKS?

9

Materials

Charcoal briquets or bricks   Self-sealing plastic bags

Pan   Water

Refrigerator freezer   Hand lens or magnifying glass

Procedure

Place a charcoal briquet or small brick in a self-sealing plastic bag. Cover the charcoal completely with water. Seal the bag and stand it in a pan to prevent spills. Let it soak overnight, and on the next day, place the bag with the soaked charcoal into the freezer. If there is room, keep the bag in the pan. Place an identical piece of charcoal in a bag by itself. Seal and place in the same pan.

Twenty-four hours later, remove the bags. Notice what has happened to the bag of charcoal and the bag of charcoal and water. Open the bags and let all the ice melt. Remove the two pieces of charcoal and compare them. Use the hand lens to examine them carefully. Look for small pieces of charcoal in the bottom of the bag with water.

Observations

What happened to the bag and the charcoal when the water froze? What was the color of the melted ice? How did freezing water affect the charcoal?

Discussion

The charcoal briquet has small air spaces. When put in water, the charcoal gets heavier because water replaces the air. When water freezes, it expands by about 10 percent. This freezing causes small pieces of the charcoal to crumble, thereby creating an uneven surface.

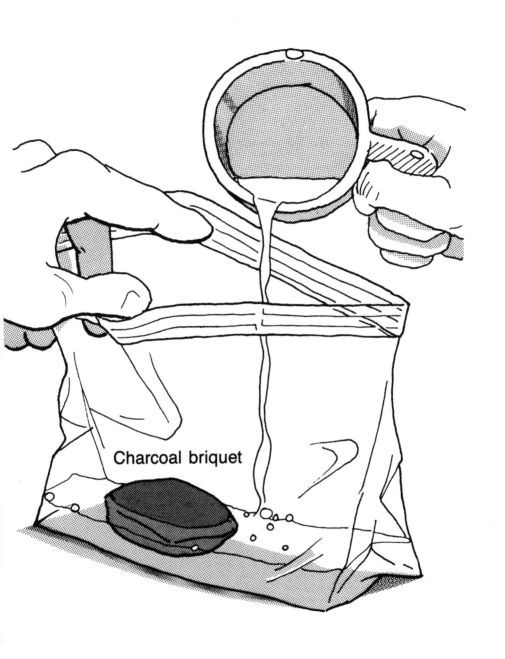

Charcoal briquet

The same thing happens with rocks in nature. Water collects in the cracks, and when the water freezes, it causes the crack to get larger. Over time, rocks can be broken apart due just to the freezing action of water. The cracks that occur in highways and driveways are enlarged by the freezing of water. Highway repair crews try to make a smooth surface by repairing the cracks in order to prevent further breaks due to the freezing of water.

These small cracks collect soil and seeds. Once the seeds start to grow, the plants' roots further break down the rocks. A plant growing out of a rock is the result of a seed getting in and starting to grow there.

Other things to try

Repeat the experiment, using sandstone or limestone.

Weigh the charcoal before and after soaking overnight to find out how much water goes into the charcoal.

Fill a pill bottle or small glass jar full of water. Put it in a plastic bag and leave it overnight in the freezer. What happened when the water froze? Have an adult help you when you go to see what happened to this part of the experiment.

HOW CAN PLANTS BREAK ROCKS?

Materials

Potting soil	Measuring cup
Plastic gallon milk jug	Knife
Plaster of Paris	Self-sealing plastic bag
Water	Plastic pill bottle
Masking tape	

Navy beans (available at grocery stores)

Procedure

Fill the pill bottle with navy beans. Then fill the pill bottle with water to the top. Put the lid on. Wrap the masking tape around the lid and pill bottle to make a watertight seal. Place the wrapped pill bottle in a self-sealing plastic bag. Set the bag in a safe place with the pill bottle standing upright. Check the pill bottle and beans for two days.

Cut off the top two-thirds of the milk jug. Put twenty-five navy beans with 1/2 cup (about 125 ml) of water into the milk jug. Soak them overnight. Remove the beans and dump the water. Add 2 cups (about 500 ml) of potting soil to the milk jug. Place the soaked beans on the soil. Add enough water to soak the soil.

In a separate container mix up a small amount of plaster of Paris as directed on the package. Pour a thin layer less than 1/4 inch (about 0.3 cm) over the top of the soil. The layer of plaster of Paris is to represent layers of rocks. Put the container in a protected area where you can check it for several days.

After you have finished with the experiment, put the pieces of plaster of Paris in the trash and dump the soil where an adult recommends.

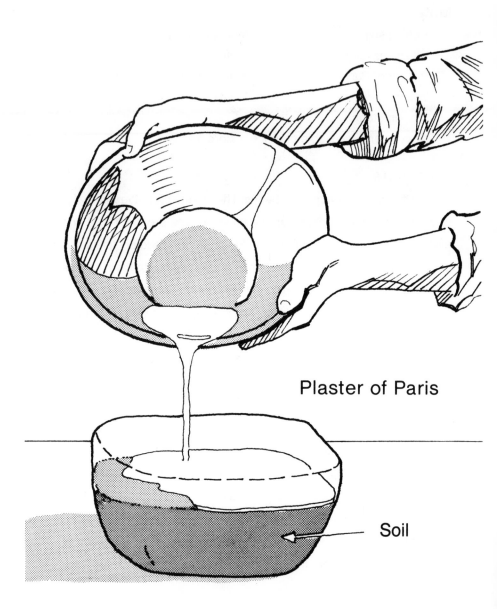

Plaster of Paris

Soil

Observations

What happened to the pill bottle with the beans? How many of the beans in the pill bottle started to grow? What happened to the layer of plaster of Paris? Were all areas of the plaster of Paris broken?

Discussion

As the beans start to grow, they absorb water, which causes them to swell and the pill bottle to break. Large seeds such as beans will often cause the soil to bulge where the bean is starting to grow.

The growing beans also are able to break the thin layer of plaster of Paris. The same thing happens where a seed lands in a crack of a rock. Once there is enough water for it to start to grow, it pushes against the rocks and breaks them, in the same way that the beans broke the pill bottle. As soil is blown, some will land on the growing seed, allowing it to continue to grow. Frequently, you will see a tree growing out of cracks in rocks.

As the tree grows, the roots continue to break apart the rocks, making a place for other plants to grow.

Other things to try

Repeat the pill bottle experiment. What would happen if you used only half as much water. What would happen if you used only half as many navy beans?

Repeat the pill bottle experiment, using seeds from different foods such as lima beans, squash, watermelon, corn, etc.

Repeat the plaster of Paris experiment. What would happen if there were various thicknesses over the beans? Can growing seeds break a layer of plaster of Paris more than 1 inch (about 2.5 cm) thick?

WHAT IS A SOIL PROFILE?

Materials

Spade and/or trowel

Ruler

Hand lens or magnifying glass

Procedure

Dig a hole straight down in the ground at least 15 inches deep (38 cm). An adult will need to give you permission where to dig. Notice the different color layers in the soil. If there is no color change, dig deeper. As you dig, look at the plant roots. The dark layer near the surface is called topsoil. The lighter color that is below the topsoil is called subsoil. If there are no layers, the soil has been mixed, which happens when they build homes. You will then need to dig in another location. Measure the depth of topsoil and subsoil. Under the subsoil is a layer of rock that's called bedrock.

Squeeze a moist sample of topsoil, then a moist sample of subsoil. Using the hand lens, compare the topsoil and subsoil. The side view from the top of the ground to the bedrock is called a soil profile. Replace the soil in the hole you dug, making sure that the topsoil is on the top.

Observations

Which is the thickest layer, the topsoil or the subsoil? If you have bedrock in your soil profile, what is the depth of the topsoil and subsoil? Which has a more gritty feel, topsoil or subsoil? How does the color of the topsoil compare with the color of the subsoil? How do the topsoil and subsoil feel? Smell? Where did you find the most plant roots? How deep is the longest root?

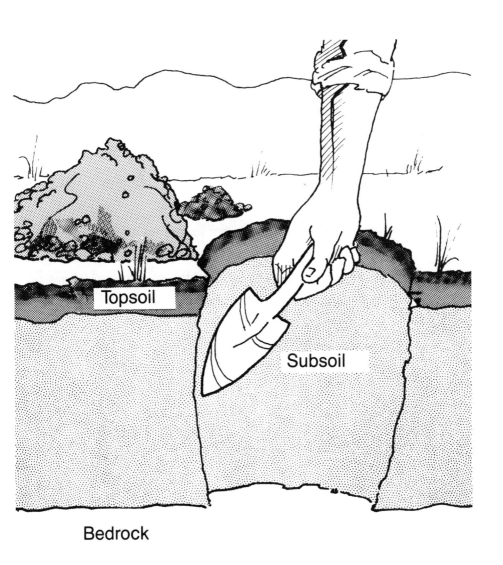

Topsoil

Subsoil

Bedrock

Discussion

A soil profile gives us information about how the soil was formed, how it should be used, and how changes have occurred. A thick layer of topsoil is good for growing plants. A dark black or brown topsoil contains dead plants that improve plant growth. The dead plants act as a plant fertilizer. A gritty feel is due to sand particles in the soil. Generally, if the subsoil is the same color as the bedrock, it was formed from the bedrock. A red or yellow color soil means that water "passes through" the soil rapidly.

Other things to try

Compare your soil profiles with other soil profiles in the same city.

Compare your soil profile with soil profiles from other areas, i.e., when on vacations. How does the depth of topsoil compare? Where different depths of topsoil occur, compare the plants growing in each place.

What happens when you add water to topsoil and subsoil?

WHAT ARE THE PROPERTIES OF SOIL? **12**

Materials

Potting soil   Sandbox sand

Several samples of soil   Several sheets of paper

Hand lens or magnifying glass

Procedure

Spread out a handful of potting soil on a piece of paper. Its dark color indicates <u>organic matter</u> (dead plants). Use the hand lens to examine the soil particles.

Spread out a handful of sandbox <u>sand</u> on another sheet of paper. Examine the size of the sand particles. The size is important since other soil particles (clay and silt) are smaller than sand particles. Sand, silt, and clay are classified by geologists according to their metric size. Sand particles are at least 2 millimeters in diameter, <u>silt</u> particles are between 1/16 and 2 millimeters in diameter, and <u>clay</u> refers to all particles that are less than 1/16 of a millimeter. Using the hand lens, examine the edges of the sand particles. Typically, sand found near a river, a lake, or an ocean has been worn smooth by the moving water.

Sometimes you will find small animals (earthworms, insects, etc.) in your soil sample.

Spread each soil sample on different sheets of paper. Examine each soil sample for the following properties: the amount of organic matter (in comparison to potting soil), the size of particles (in comparison to sand particles), shape of the edges, the way it feels, and the presence of living things.

Squeeze a moist sample of soil between your fingers. If it feels

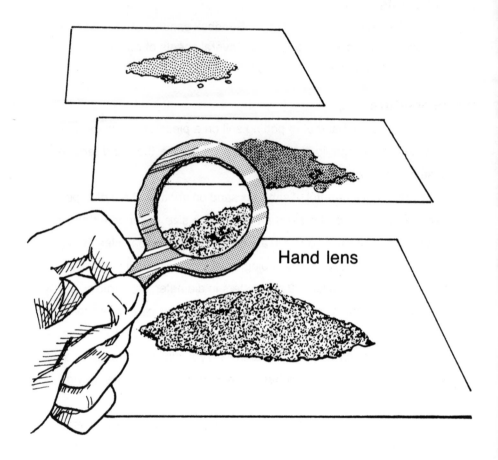

Hand lens

gritty, there is a great deal of sand, but if it feels smooth, it contains a great deal of clay. Determine the most common type of soil (sand or clay) in each soil sample.

Observations

Which soil sample has the greatest amount of organic matter? Which soil sample has the smallest soil particles? Which soil sample has the smoothest particles? Which soil sample has the most sand? Clay? Which animals did you find in the soil samples?

Discussion

In this experiment you compared specific properties in different samples of soil. Geologists have found that soil varies from place to place, and they always describe it based upon the amount of organic matter, the amount of sand, silt, and/or clay, the smoothness of soil particles, and the living matter in the soil (both plant and animals). Generally, the darker the soil, the greater the amount of organic material. The dark color is due to recently decayed plants and animals. More organic material in a soil typically results in better plant growth because the organic matter is a fertilizer.

The smaller the soil particles, the slower the water moves through the soil. Typically, water will move faster through sand than through clay or silt because there is more space between sand particles than between clay particles. This space allows for easier water movement.

Other things to try

Compare your soil samples with samples from other parts of the country.

Which type of soil sample do earthworms prefer?

Put different soil samples in a paper cup. Punch holes in the bottom of the cup with a pin and then add 1/4 cup (about 60 ml) of water. With a container under the cup, measure which sample allows the most and the least water to pass through the soil. Which type of soil has the slowest water movement?

HOW MUCH WATER CAN SOIL HOLD?   **13**

Materials

Pieces of old washcloths   Rubberbands

Measuring cup   Bucket

Two pans   Newspaper

Masking tape

Two 46-ounce juice cans, both ends removed

Different types of soil, such as potting soil and sand

Procedure

If not outside, cover your area with newspaper. Wrap the pieces of washcloth over one end of each can. Hold it in place with rubberbands. Then tape the edges of the cloth around the cans. Put the covered end of each juice can into separate pans. Slowly add 2 cups (about 500 ml) of sand to one juice can and 2 cups (about 500 ml) of potting soil to the other juice can. Gently shake the cans so soil is at the same height. Slowly pour 1 cup (about 250 ml) of water into each juice can. After five minutes, carefully remove the cans and set them in a bucket. Measure and record how much water passed through the sand and the potting soil into the pans. Pour the water and the soil onto the ground in a place recommended by an adult because the mixture could plug the sink.

Observations

How much water went through the sand? How much water went through the potting soil? Which type of soil had the most water that passed through it? How does the water look in the cake pans? Which pan has the most soil that came through the washcloth? Which plan has the clearer water?

Washcloth

Discussion

The space between the soil particles contains air that is used by earthworms and often soil insects. When it rains, the water goes into these spaces.

Water moves through different soils at different speeds. Geologists have found that the larger the soil particles (i.e., sand), the faster the water passes through the soil. Sand particles are uneven, so they don't fit close together to prevent water from passing through. When there is a puddle of water in your yard, the soil probably has small particles which result in slower water movement. For crops to grow, the soil must hold onto some of the water. But for a football or a soccer field, you want the water to pass through rapidly. Therefore, you will probably find these fields have a sandy soil. Geologists will frequently describe a soil as porous or not porous. They are referring to the soil's porosity or the amount of air space between the soil particles

Other things to try

Repeat the experiment, using topsoil and subsoil. Compare the effects. How much water passes through in thirty minutes? What happens when you use 2 cups (about 500 ml) of water?

What happens when you use 3 cups (about 750 ml) of soil and 3 cups (about 750 ml) of water?

How does hand packing the potting soil compare with leaving the potting soil loose?

HOW FAST DOES WATER GO THROUGH SOIL?

14

Materials

Measuring cup

Watch with a second hand

Water

Masking tape

Three wide-mouth jars that you can easily put your hand inside

Different types of soil, such as potting soil and sand

Procedure

Put 2 cups (about 500 ml) of sand in one jar, 2 cups (about 500 ml) of potting soil in another jar, and 1 cup (about 250 ml) of sand and 1 cup (about 250 ml) of potting soil mixed in the third jar. Label each jar with its soil type. With your hand, gently pack the soil in each jar. Add 1 cup (about 250 ml) of water to each jar, timing how long it takes for all the water to sink into the soil. After finishing, dump the soil in a place recommended by an adult.

Observations

How long did it take for all of the water to sink into each soil? Which type of soil soaked up the water first? How did the jar with sand the jar with potting soil compare with the other jar that had both?

Discussion

The type of soil affects how fast water soaks into it. Permeability is the rate at which water goes through soil. Geologists describe soils where water passes through quickly as being permeable. Generally, the more firmly packed the soil, the slower water soaks in. In sandy soils, water goes through faster than through other soils; therefore, it has a high permeability because some soil particles, like clay, fit more

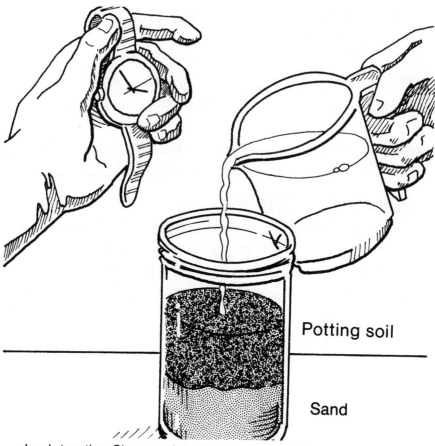

Potting soil

Sand

closely together. Since sand particles have rounded corners that leave air spaces, water moves rapidly through these air spaces.

Other things to try

Repeat the experiment, but do not pack the soil. How does the result compare with that of the packed soils?

Repeat the experiment, using soil with growing grass. How does soil with grass compare with soil without grass?

Before dumping, put the soils in the sun. What happens after two hours? Two days?

WHAT PATTERNS DO SEDIMENTS   **15**
MAKE IN WATER?

Materials

Large peanut-butter jar with tight-fitting lid
Samples of potting soil and light-colored sand
Water
Hand lens or magnifying glass

Procedure

Using a hand lens, examine and record the color and particle size (coarse, fine, etc.) of each type of soil. Add three handfuls of each kind of soil to the jar. Fill the jar three-fourths full with water. Put the lid on tightly. Gently shake the jar of water and soil 100 times. Set the jar in a place where it won't be moved for one day. Observe every half hour for three hours. Then look at the jar the next morning.

After finishing your observations, dump the contents of your jar where an adult tells you. Rinse the jar outside because soil can plug the sink.

Observations

What were the color and particle size of each type of soil? After shaking the soil and water, what color was the water? After thirty minutes, what is floating on the top? What is happening after one, two, and three hours? The next day, what color is the water? The next day, what is the color of the soil at the bottom? What is the color of the next layer of <u>sediments</u> (soil that falls out of water)? What is the color of the top layer? What size are the sediments at the bottom of the jar? What size are the sediments at the top layer of the jar? Are the soil layers the same thickness? If not, which is the thickest?

Soil

Discussion

Moving water is able to carry soil. Geologists have found that large amounts and fast-moving water can carry more soil than small amounts or slow-moving water. Whenever the moving water slows down, it isn't able to carry the soil any further. The heavier soil particles (sand) are the first to be deposited, or to fall out of the moving water. The smaller soil particles (potting soil) can be carried farther by the water because they are lighter. This pattern—heavy soil particles deposited first and the light soil particles being deposited last—occurs with all water-carried soil. When a small stream enters a bigger stream, the moving water slows down. Most of the soil being carried is deposited, the heaviest soil particles being deposited first. The bottom of lakes, ponds, rivers, and oceans have sediments that have been carried by moving water. After thousands of years, these sediments turn into <u>sedimentary rock</u>.

Other things to try

Continue observing the jar until the water is clear.

Repeat the experiment, using six handfuls of sand and only three handfuls of another soil.

HOW DOES SLOPE AFFECT SOIL EROSION?

Materials

Soil

Two large shallow pans

Sprinkler can

Two quart-size cardboard milk cartons

Four wood blocks (same size) or bricks

Measuring cup

Masking tape

Procedure

Cut away one side of each milk carton lengthwise. Tape the open spouts shut. Using the measuring cup, fill the cartons with equal amounts of soil.

It is best to do the filling outside because soil can clog the sink. Prop one end of one carton on one block. The carton is now sloped like a hill. Place three blocks under one end of the other carton. Notice the slope or angle of the cartons by looking at them from the side. Notice the very steep slope of the carton propped on three blocks. Place a large shallow pan below the non-propped edge of each carton to collect the runoff (water not held by the soil). Pour 2 cups (about 500 ml) of water into the sprinkler can and gently pour this amount on the carton with one block. Pour the same amount on the carton with three blocks. Notice what happens to the water and soil. Measure how much water ran off each milk carton.

Dump the soil where an adult tells you.

Observations

Which slope of the carton lost the most soil (ended up in the pan)? Which slope of the carton lost the least soil? Which slope of the carton

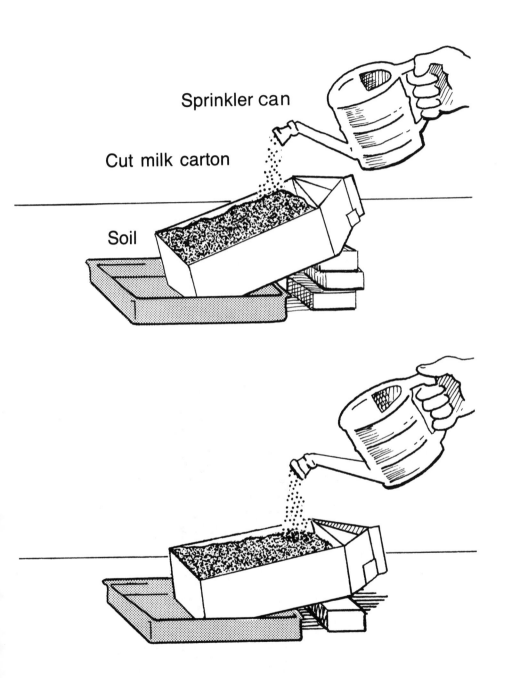

Sprinkler can

Cut milk carton

Soil

had the fastest runoff of water? Which slope absorbed the most water? How does slope affect erosion?

Discussion

Rain can carry soil from one area to another. This process is called erosion. Geologists know that faster-moving water can carry more soil. The steeper the slope of the soil, the faster the water moves. When water moves quickly, there is more soil erosion. Therefore, geologists try to slow down the fast-moving water by using plants, diverting water in several directions, blocking it like a dam, or a combination of these. The soil particles will be carried until the speed of the moving water cannot carry them. Then they are deposited, or dropped.

When farmers plant furrow crops like corn or beans on slopes, they plant around the hill. Planting up and down the hill causes more soil erosion because the water follows the vertical furrows. Planting around the hill (horizontal furrows) slows down the moving water. Typically, farmers will grow hay crops on steeply sloped land to try and prevent soil erosion.

Other things to try

Repeat the experiment, using two blocks. Compare the results with those in which one and three blocks were used.

Repeat the experiment, using one carton in which you have grown grass. How does the grass affect runoff with different slopes?

Repeat the experiment, comparing vertical and horizontal furrows made with a fork.

Repeat the experiment, comparing fast and slow rain of the same amount. Hint: A fast rain would be the emptying of the sprinkler can as fast as possible.

HOW DO PLANTS AFFECT EROSION?

Materials

Two half-gallon-size cardboard milk cartons
Soil
Grass seed or transplanted grass
Two wood blocks (same size) or bricks
Two large shallow pans
Measuring cup
Masking tape
Sprinkler can

Procedure

Cut away one side of each of the milk cartons lengthwise. Tape the ends shut. Fill the cartons with equal amounts of soil. Plant grass seed only in one carton, and water each container daily with equal amounts of water. Once the grass is at least 2 inches (5 cm) tall (about two weeks), you are ready to determine how plants affect erosion. You can also, with an adult's permission, dig up soil with grass already growing.

Now take your equipment outside because soil can clog the sink. Prop one edge of each container on a block. The containers are now sloped like a hill. Place a large shallow pan at the bottom end of each milk carton to collect the water that runs off. Using the sprinkler can, pour 2 cups (about 500 ml) of water gently on each container. Measure the amount of water and soil that ran off each carton.

When finished, dump the milk cartons where an adult tells you and clean up the area.

Observations

Which milk carton had the most water (runoff) that went into the

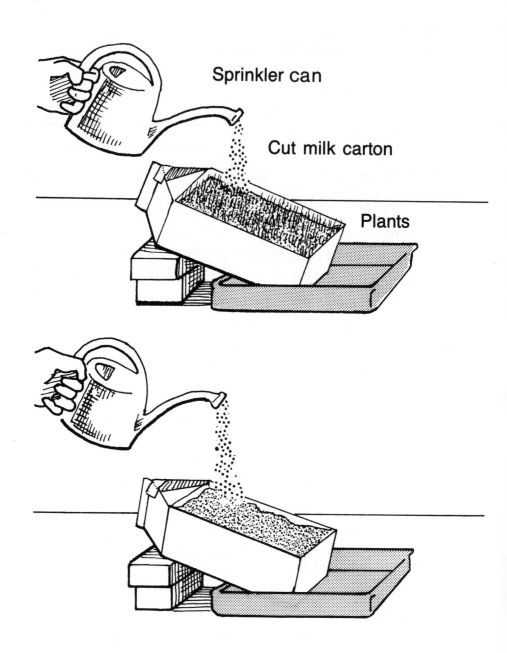

Sprinkler can

Cut milk carton

Plants

pan? Which milk carton had the slowest runoff? Which milk carton had the most erosion? Which milk carton lost the most soil?

Discussion

Rain can carry soil from one area to another area. Geologists are always trying to prevent the loss of soil since it takes almost 1,000 years for nature to make one inch of topsoil. Plant roots tend to hold soil in place and slow soil erosion, although very heavy rain can still erode planted soil.

Without plants, the steeper the slope, the more soil erosion will occur. The smaller the soil particles, the easier for the moving water to erode the soil. Sometimes, it is difficult to get new grass to grow on steep slopes. Typically, farmers will grow hay crops on steeply sloped land to prevent soil erosion. Hay crops do not require the turning over of the soil, and the roots help hold the soil particles in place. Hay crops will survive winters like the grass in your yard.

Other things to try

Repeat the experiment, using different sized blocks under each carton to create different heights. Compare the effects. Which has the deepest erosion patterns? Compare the erosion of different types of soils.

HOW DOES WIND CAUSE SOIL EROSION?

18

Materials

Potting soil	Sand
Small gravel	Large balloon
Ruler	Measuring cup
Bucket .	

Procedure

Mix together 1 cup (about 250 ml) each of potting soil, sand, and small gravel. Pile the mixture on the ground about 3 feet (about 1 m) from the wall of a building. Blow up the balloon, holding the air inside with your fingers. Lay the balloon, still closed by your fingers, about 6 inches (15 cm) from the pile. The balloon will become our wind. Holding the balloon in place, let the air out while pointing it at the pile of soil. Observe where the potting soil, sand, and gravel have been blown. Measure how far they have moved.

Clean up the area and dispose of the materials in a place specified by an adult.

Observations

Which materials were moved the farthest by the wind? Which materials were moved the least by the wind? How did the size of a particle affect the distance it traveled?

Discussion

Winds are able to move large quantities of soil from one place to another.

After a rain, the muddy sidewalks could be due to the mixing of rain with the soil particles previously blown onto the sidewalk. When

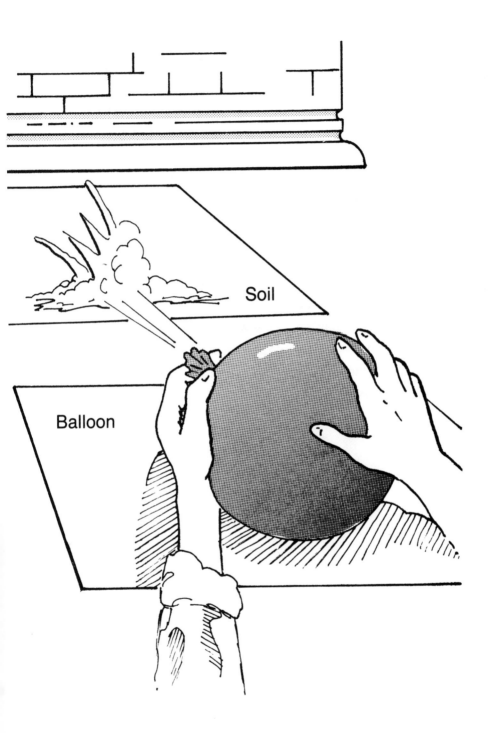

Soil

Balloon

the soil particles are wet, they are heavier; therefore, they will not be moved as easily. Once the wet soil dries out, it will be easier for the wind to move it to another place. The lightweight particles (potting soil) will be blown farther than the heavier pieces. The pieces of gravel will be moved the least. Strong winds are able to blow things farther. Geologists have found that the smaller the soil particles, the easier they are to move. Even a gentle breeze can blow very small pieces of soil from one place to another.

Other things to try

Repeat the experiment, placing the balloon twice as far from the pile. What was the effect?

What would happen if there were stronger winds?

Look for evidence of erosion caused by the wind in your neighborhood. Is there any area that has more erosion caused by the wind than other areas?

HOW DOES A RAINDROP CAUSE EROSION?

19

Materials

Pie pan	Soil
Medicine dropper	Large sheets of white paper
Ruler	

Procedure

Fill a pie pan with soil. Press the soil down until it lies even with the pan's edges. Put the pie pan in the middle of a sheet of large white paper. Fill the medicine dropper with water. Position the dropper 3 feet (about 1 m) above the center of the soil. Let several drops fall on the soil. Measure how far the soil splashes from the pie pan. This is called splash erosion.

Using a new sheet of white paper, repeat the experiment. This time, drop the water from a height of 6 feet (about 2 m). Measure how far the soil splashes from the pan.

Observations

Where was the most soil splashed? How did the dropping height affect the amount of soil splashed?

Discussion

A falling raindrop hits the soil with a tremendous force. As with anything, the larger the raindrop, the greater its hitting force; the farther an object falls, the greater its hitting force. Even when water was dropped a short distance, soil was splashed out of the pie pan. Splash erosion can be reduced by growing plants. Raindrops bounce off plants, thereby creating a shorter falling distance to the soil and causing a weaker splash. When the exposed soil is on a hill, there is

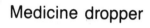
Medicine dropper

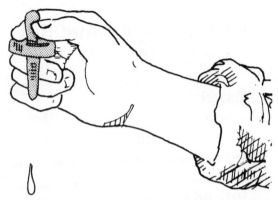

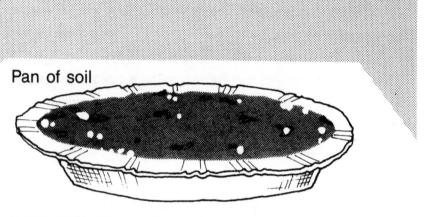
Pan of soil

greater erosion because the moving water will carry the loose soil caused by splash erosion.

Other things to try

Repeat the experiment, comparing soil with growing grass to soil without grass.

Place a pencil in the path of the water. What happens to the amount of splash?

After a rain, look for evidence of splash erosion around the sides of buildings.

Compare the effects of splash erosion on different types of soil.

HOW STRONG IS THAT ACID?

Materials

pH paper and color chart (available at aquarium/pet shops)

Small plastic/glass jars

Tweezers

Common household liquids such as orange juice, apple juice, vinegar, tap water, window cleaner, liquid detergent, dissolved baking soda in a small amount of water, lemon juice, tomato juice, cranberry juice, milk of magnesia, bleach, soft drinks, etc.

Procedure

Put a small amount of one of the liquids in a jar. Using tweezers, dip a small piece of pH paper into the sample. Remove it. Immediately compare the color of the pH paper with the color chart. Record the pH value for the liquid. Using a fresh piece of pH paper each time, repeat the test for each liquid.

Throw the used pieces of the pH paper into the garbage and dump liquids down the sink. Rinse the jars.

Observation

Which liquid has the lowest pH (strongest acid)? Which liquid has the highest pH (strongest base)? How do the different juices that you could drink at breakfast compare for pH?

Discussion

Acids and bases are chemicals that we use each day. We have many of them in our homes. The acid in foods gives them a sour taste. The stronger the acid, the more sour the taste. Common household acid foods are vinegar, citrus fruit juice, and tomatoes. The chemical opposite of acids is bases. Baking soda is one of the most common

pH paper

bases we have in our homes. When acids and bases are mixed together, they neutralize each other.

The pH scale, which measures the amount of acid in substances, goes from 0 to 14. Distilled (pure) water is neutral (not an acid or base), and its pH is 7. Values that are lower than 7 are acids, and those higher than 7 are bases.

Geologists are interested in how acids like acid rain affect soil, buildings, layers of rocks, and lakes and rivers. Acid rain is a serious problem in the northeastern United States and in eastern Canada. Rain becomes more acidic when air pollution from factories and cars mixes with it.

Other things to try

Compare the pH of a sour apple and a sweet apple. Which of the household liquids is the closest to the pH of acid rain (pH less than 5.6)?

WHAT IS ACID RAIN?

Materials

Small plastic/glass jars   Tweezers
pH paper and color chart (available at aquarium/pet shops)
Samples of rain, distilled water, and tap water

Procedure

Put a small amount of distilled water in a jar. Using tweezers, dip a small piece of pH paper into the sample. Remove it. Immediately compare the color of the pH paper with the color chart. Then do the same for rain and tap water, using a fresh piece of pH paper each time. If the pH is less than a 5.6, it is called acid rain. Compare the pH of rain collected early in a storm with that collected at the end of the storm.

Throw the used pieces of the pH paper in the garbage and dump the liquids down the sink. Wash the jars and rinse them with distilled water before using them again.

Observations

Which liquid was the closest to being neutral (pH = 7)? Which liquid has the lowest pH (strongest acid)? Does the early part or the end of the storm have the lowest pH?

Discussion

Geologists have found that exhausts from cars and trucks and from the burning of coal combines with water vapor to form acids. When it rains, the result is called acid rain. It includes forms of rain, snow, sleet, hail, and fog that fall to earth. Acid rain affects lakes; the water gets too acidic for fish, snails, etc., to live in.

Typically, rain released at the start of a storm is usually more acidic

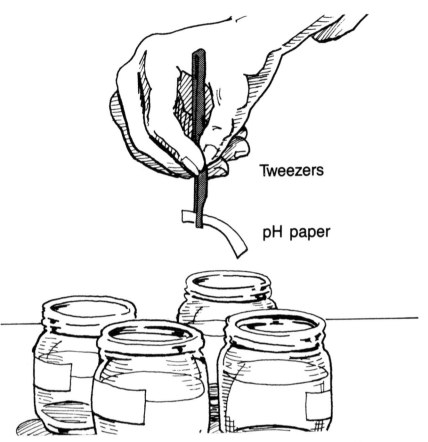

Tweezers

pH paper

than rain near the end of a storm. The same pattern occurs with snow. The most acid rain measured came during a storm in Wheeling, West Virginia. It had a pH of less than 2.0. Some weather stations report the pH of storms. Check the weather report in your local newspaper.

Other things to try

Compare the pH of hot and cold tap water.

Collect some snow, let it melt, and then determine its pH.

Compare the pH of rain collected during the second day of a storm with that collected on the first day of the storm.

HOW DOES THE pH SCALE WORK? 22

Materials

Adding machine tape at least 15 meters long
Metric ruler (use the metric side of a regular ruler)
Red marking pen

Procedures

This experiment uses only metric measurements to make it easier to understand how the pH scale works.

Unroll the adding machine tape. Measure 1 meter from the right end of the tape. Draw a line across the tape and label it pH 7. On the left side of the line, measure 10 millimeters from the pH 7 line and draw another line. Label this pH 6. On the left side of the pH 6 line, measure 100 millimeters (10 cm) and draw the pH 5 line. Continue on the left side of pH 5, measure 1,000 millimeters (100 cm or 1 m), and label this line pH 4. Continuing on the left side of the pH 4 line, measure ten times the distance from pH 5 to pH 4. Your line for pH 3 is 10 meters from pH 4.

Label to the right of pH 7 as a base and left of pH 7 as an acid.

Observations

How much more acidic is a liquid of pH 4 than a liquid of pH 5? How much more acidic is a liquid of pH 4 than a liquid of pH 6? How much more acidic is a liquid of pH 4 than a liquid of pH 7?

Discussion

The amount of acid or base is shown by the pH scale, which is based upon multiples of ten. The pH 3 is 10 times more acidic than a pH 4, 100 (10 x 10) times more acidic than ph 5, 1,000 (10 x 10 x 10)

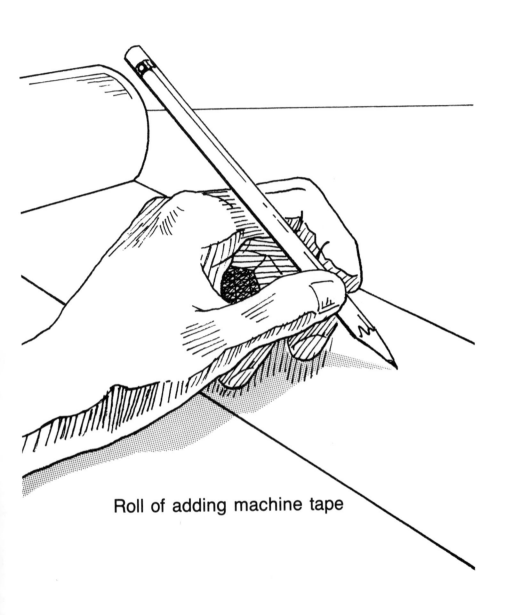

Roll of adding machine tape

times more acidic than pH 6, and 10,000 (10 x 10 x 10 x 10) times more acidic than pH 7.

The pH scale allows geologists to compare the amount of acid in different materials, which they can then report to the people. People with swimming pools check the pH of the water to determine how much chlorine to add.

Other things to try

Label the following liquids on your tape:

Distilled water pH 7.0

Milk pH 6.6

Tomato juice pH 4.2

Normal rain pH 5.6 and higher

Acid rain pH 5.6 and lower.

WHAT IS THE pH OF SOIL? **23**

Materials

Distilled water and tap water

Different types of soil, such as potting soil, sand, and
    garden soil

pH paper and color chart (available at aquarium/pet shops)

Several small jars with lids such as baby-food jars

Powdered lime (available at garden stores)

Measuring spoons

Procedure

Put some distilled water in a jar. Tear off a small strip of pH paper. Dip end of tape into the distilled water. Match the color of the tape to the pH chart. Repeat, adding tap water to another jar. Each time you test, use a new strip of test tape.

Fill a jar half full with potting soil. Now, fill the jar almost full with distilled water. Fasten lid securely and shake for thirty seconds. Remove the lid and wait for ten minutes. Touch the pH paper to the soil water and read the pH value. Repeat the procedure with other soils.

Put 1/4 teaspoon of lime in a jar half filled with distilled water. Tighten lid and shake. Then test with a strip of pH paper. Add 1/4 teaspoon of lime to each soil sample. Cap and shake. After ten minutes, repeat the pH test.

Dump the soil in the proper place. Rinse the jars outside before cleaning them in the sink because soil can plug up your sink. Throw the used pH papers into the garbage.

Observations

How did the pH of the tap water compare with the pH of distilled

Soil

water? What was the pH of the soils you tested? How does lime affect the pH?

Discussion

The lower the number on the pH paper means it is more acidic (like vinegar). The higher the number of the pH paper means it is more basic (like baking soda). A pH of 7 means it is neutral, neither acidic or basic.

Plants grow best in soil that meets their specific pH needs. Forests and damp areas usually have acidic soils. Sandy soil and desert soil usually are basic. Geologists use the pH of soil to help describe the overall conditions of a region.

When the soil is too acidic for certain crops, farmers add lime to make the soil more basic. When the soil is too acidic, the plant roots aren't as able to grow and take in water. These plants are weak and small and seldom produce food. Each year you should test your garden soil to see if you need to add lime.

Other things to try

How does the pH of light-colored soils compare with that of dark-colored soils?

How does the pH compare for topsoil and subsoil?

Do radishes grow better in acidic soil or basic soil?

Look in a seed catalog to determine the best soil pH for vegetables such as radishes, tomatoes, carrots, watermelons, beans, etc.

HOW DOES CALCIUM CARBONATE AFFECT ACID RAIN?

Materials

Two peanut-butter jars   Chalk (calcium carbonate)

White vinegar   Measuring cup

Distilled water

Hand lens or magnifying glass

pH paper and color chart (available at aquarium/pet shops)

Procedure

Put 2 cups (about 500 ml) of distilled water in one jar and 2 cups (about 500 ml) of vinegar in the other jar. Using the tweezers, dip a small piece of pH paper into the jar with distilled water. Remove it. Immediately compare the color of the pH paper with the color chart. Repeat the procedure with the vinegar. The vinegar will act as acid rain. Break three long pieces of chalk into very small pieces and put them in the water jar. Break three more long pieces of chalk into small pieces and put them in the vinegar jar. Wait one hour and then test each jar with pH paper. Record the pH of each jar. Record what you see with a hand lens at the bottom of each jar. Compare the chalk that is in each jar.

Dump the liquids down the sink and throw the chalk into the garbage.

Observations

Which jar has the most acid after one hour? What did the chalk do to the pH of the distilled water? What did the chalk do to the pH of the vinegar?

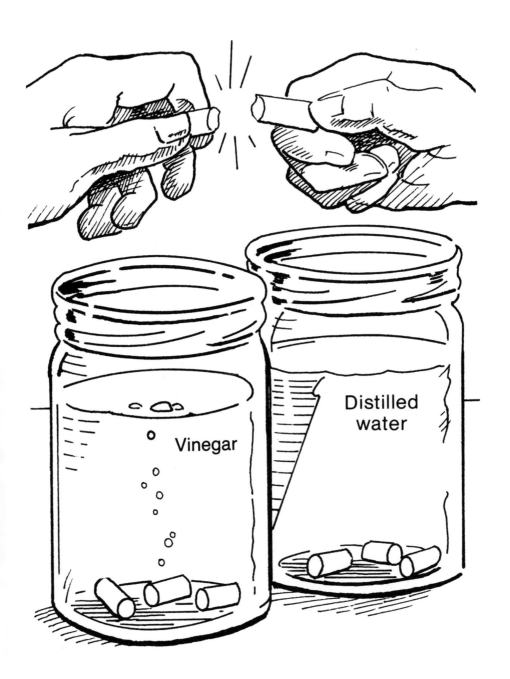

Vinegar

Distilled
water

Discussion

Geologists have wondered why certain areas are more affected by acid rain than are other areas. One of the things geologists found was that certain rocks neutralized the acid rain. These rocks always contained calcium carbonate. Chalk is a soft type of calcium carbonate. When calcium carbonate rocks are powdered, the result is frequently called lime. When lime is added to soil and water, it raises its pH (makes it less acidic). However, this procedure must be done every year because more acid rain is continually falling. It takes a large quantity of calcium carbonate to neutralize a small amount of acid rain. Therefore, if a large lake is acidic, each year large amounts of calcium carbonate would have to be added. This is a very expensive solution to the problem of acid rain.

Other things to try

Predict what would happen to the chalk and what would be the pH if you used half vinegar and half distilled water. Test your prediction.

What happens when you use lemon juice rather than vinegar?

What happens to the pH when you see you use only half a piece of chalk in the vinegar?

HOW CAN WE WEAKEN ACID RAIN? **25**

Materials

Lemonade mix	Distilled water
Measuring cup	Pitcher
Plastic cups	Tweezers

pH paper color chart (available at aquarium/pet shops)

Procedure

Using the tweezers, dip a small piece of the pH paper into a cup of distilled water. Remove the paper and immediately compare it with the color chart. Record the pH value for the distilled water. Discard the distilled water.

Using distilled water, mix the lemonade as directed on the package. Measure 1/4 cup (about 60 ml) of the prepared lemonade; add 1/4 cup (about 60 ml) of distilled water. Predict whether the pH of this sample will be higher or lower than that of the distilled water. Test its pH and record the value.

Measure 1/4 cup (about 60 ml) of prepared lemonade; add 2 cups (about 500 ml) of distilled water. Predict whether the pH of this sample will be higher than the previous test or lower. Test your prediction and record the pH.

Taste each sample.

Throw the used pieces of pH paper in the garbage. Rinse the cups and follow an adult's suggestions about the lemonade.

Observations

Which sample had the lowest pH (most acid)? Which sample was closest to the pH of distilled water? How does adding water influence the pH? What causes some lemonades to taste better than others?

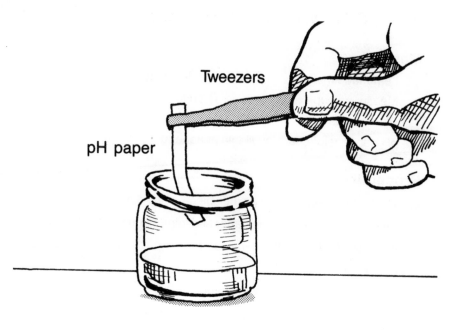

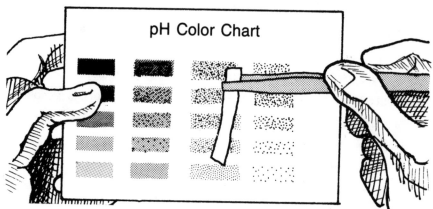

How does the pH of each sample compare with acid rain (pH less than 5.6)?

Discussion

Acids and bases are used every day of our lives. They are commonly found in our homes. Common acidic foods are vinegar and lemon juice. Baking soda is an example of a common household base. Sometimes rain contains some acid and is called acid rain.

Acid rain is one of the big problems of the world. It affects plants and animals by harming the places they inhabit. There are three major ways to weaken acid rain. One is to neutralize it by adding a base such as calcium carbonate (lime). A second method is to add water that has a pH close to that of distilled water, thereby diluting (weakening) the acid rain. Another method is to prevent acid rain from occurring in the future by reducing the amount of exhausts from cars and trucks and burning less coal.

In this experiment, you found that adding distilled water to the lemonade raised its pH (made it less acidic). This procedure is similar to the second method. Imagine how much distilled water it would take to dilute the Great Lakes if they were as acidic as your original prepared lemonade.

Other things to try

Use the sample containing 1/4 cup (about 60 ml) of prepared lemonade and 2 cups (about 500 ml) of distilled water. Take 1/4 cup (about 60 ml) of this weak lemonade and add an additional 1/4 cup (about 60 ml) of distilled water. Predict the pH of this sample. Test your prediction.

How does mixing up lemonade with only half the recommended water affect its pH?

What happens to the pH when you add baking soda to lemonade?

HOW DOES ACID RAIN AFFECT PLANTS?

Materials

Radish seeds

White vinegar

Chalk

Self-sealing plastic bags

Stapler

Paper towels

Measuring cup

Masking tape

Distilled water

pH paper and color chart (available at aquarium/pet shops)

Procedure

Fold three paper towels to fit flat in each of the three self-sealing plastic bags. Punch staples all the way across each bag about one-third up from the bottom. Add 20 radish seeds to each bag. Most of the seeds will stay above the staples. Label each bag with the type of liquid that will be added: distilled water, vinegar, and vinegar with chalk. Test each liquid with the pH paper using procedures from earlier activities. For bag one, add 1/2 cup (about 125 ml) of distilled water. For bag two, add 1/2 cup (about 125 ml) vinegar. For bag three, add 1/2 cup (about 125 ml) vinegar to which two large pieces of powdered chalk have been added. Seal each bag. Hang the bags up with masking tape in a sunny place recommended by an adult.

Check daily to see what happens to the seeds in each bag. Continue this procedure for two weeks. If a paper towel appears to be dry, add 1/4 cup (about 60 ml) of the appropriate liquid.

Observations

Which liquid had the most acid? Which liquid had the most seeds that started to grow (germinate)? After two weeks, which plants are the healthiest looking?

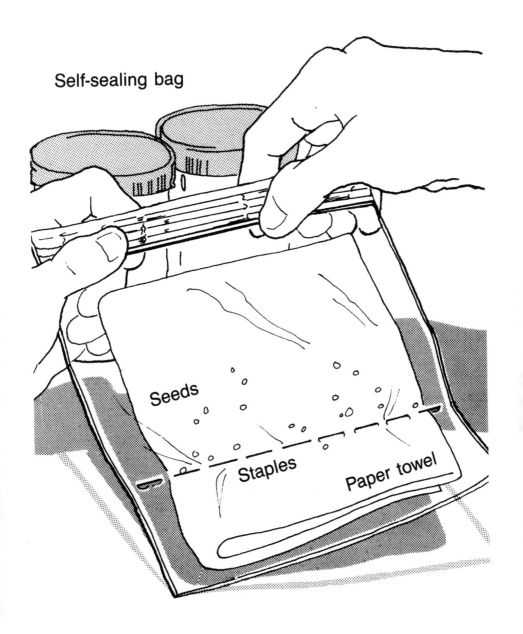

Self-sealing bag

Seeds

Staples

Paper towel

Discussion

Acid rain tends to block the roots of plants so that they are unable to take nutrients from the soil. Different types of plants grow best in the pH range that meets their specific needs. For example, radishes grow best when the pH is between 6 and 8 while maple tree seeds grow best when the pH is between 5 and 6.

People should test their lawn and garden soil to find out its pH. If the soil is too acid, they add lime (like the chalk in this experiment). The chalk neutralizes the acid rain. Acid rain makes an acid soil more acid. Lime may need to be added each year.

Other things to try

Repeat the activity, substituting different seeds such as lettuce, beans, carrots, marigolds, beets, etc. Compare these results with the radishes.

What happens when you use vinegar rather than water on flowers? Obtain a parent's permission to try this on plants such as a coleus.

WHAT HAPPENS IN AN EARTHQUAKE? **27**

Materials

Table knife

Water

Medicine dropper

Modeling clay (four different colors)

Wax paper

Ruler

Procedure

For this experiment, each layer of modeling clay is to represent a layer of rock. Flatten each color of clay into a sheet that is at least 10 inches (about 25 cm) long and 4 inches (about 10 cm) wide. Each sheet should be of a different thickness, such as 1/4, 1/2, 2/3, and 3/4 inches. Trim each sheet of clay so it is 8 inches (about 20 cm) by 3 inches (about 7.5 cm). Place a large sheet of wax paper on a flat surface. Put the 3/4-inch-thick layer of modeling clay on top of the wax paper. Using the medicine dropper, sprinkle several drops of water over the top of this layer. Gently place the 1/4-inch-thick layer of modeling clay on top of the 3/4-inch-thick layer. Using the table knife, cut across only the 1/4-inch-thick layer at a 45-degree angle. This cut represents a fault (cracks in rocks where they can move). Again, sprinkle several drops of water on top of the 1/4-inch-thick layer of clay. Next, put the 2/3-inch-thick layer on top. Sprinkle several drops of water before adding the 1/2-inch-thick layer.

Put one hand on each end of the stack of modeling clay. Push toward the middle. Notice the general shape of the layers. Record what happens to the 1/4-inch-layer with the fault.

Observations

What was the general shape after being pressed together? How tall was your mountain? What happened to the layer with the fault?

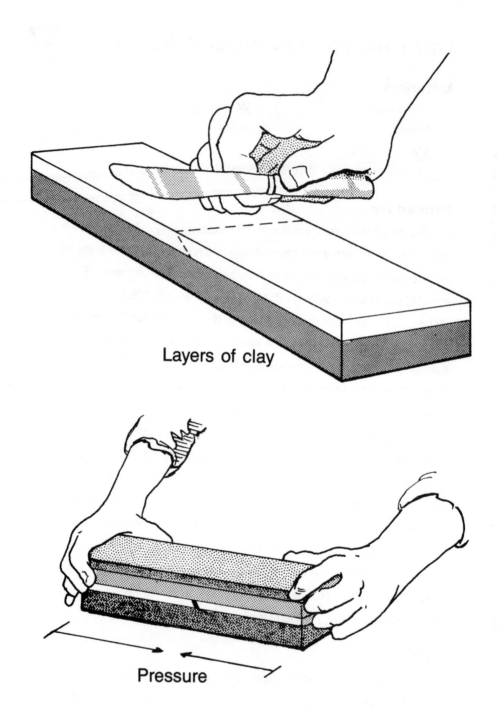

Layers of clay

Pressure

Discussion

The crust of the earth is made of many layers of rocks, which vary in thickness. In this experiment, clay was used to represent the layers of rocks. When you pushed the ends together, you caused an earthquake. When the layers of clay without a fault were pushed toward one another, they buckled in the center. This bending of rocks is called a fold. Geologists believe that many mountains are formed in this way. However, when there is a fault, the layers will slide along the cut. When layers of rock shift, slide, and/or buckle, there is a shaking of the earth. This shaking is called an earthquake, and its vibrations are measured by a sensitive instrument called a seismograph. The greater the movement in the layers of rock, the stronger the vibrations and the more severe the earthquake. The movements of rocks can occur near or far from the surface.

Other things to try

Repeat the experiment with faults in two layers. How does the pattern compare? What happens when there are two faults in the same layer?

Repeat the experiment without a fault, using carpet samples or colored bath towels. How does the height of the mountain compare?

WHAT IS A 5.4 EARTHQUAKE?

28

Materials

Metric ruler   Pencil/pen

Adding machine tape (at least 14 meters long)

Procedure

The strength of an earthquake is reported on the <u>Richter scale</u>. The higher the Richter number, the stronger the earthquake. This experiment uses only metric measurements to make it easier to understand the Richter scale. To develop a model of the Richter scale, unroll the adding machine tape. Draw a line across the tape near the left end. Label this 2.4. On the right side of the line, measure 10 millimeters from the 2.4 line and draw another line. Label this line 3.4. On the right side of the 3.4 line, measure 100 millimeters (10 cm), and

Roll of adding machine tape

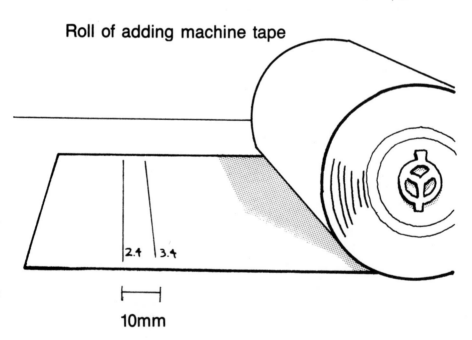

2.4   3.4

10mm

draw the 4.4 line. On the right side of the 4.4 line, measure 1,000 millimeters (100 cm or 1 m), and label this line 5.4. Measure 10 meters on the right side of the 5.4 line, and label it 6.4.

Observations

How much stronger is a 3.4 earthquake than a 2.4? How much stronger is a 4.4 earthquake than a 2.4? How much stronger is a 5.4 earthquake than a 2.4?

Discussion

Geologists use the Richter scale to measure the amount of energy released when an earthquake occurs. The Richter scale is based upon multiples of ten. A 6.4 earthquake is 10 times stronger than a 5.4, 100 (10 x 10) times stronger than a 4.4 earthquake, 1,000 (10 x 10 x 10) times stronger than a 3.4, and 10,000 (10 x 10 x 10 x 10) times stronger than a 2.4 earthquake.

The famous San Francisco earthquake of 1906 had a Richter value of 8.3. A 2.4 earthquake would cause a hanging plant to swing slightly. A 3.4 earthquake would cause dishes, windows, and doors to rattle as if a heavy truck were passing by. A 5.4 earthquake causes walls to crack, and people find it difficult to stand. A 6.4 earthquake causes buildings to collapse, underground pipes to break, and large cracks to appear in the ground.

Other things to try

Look up earthquakes in reference sources and label on your tape the Richter value of famous earthquakes. How much longer a piece of tape would you need to represent a 7.4 earthquake?

HOW DO STALACTITES AND STALAGMITES FORM IN CAVES?

29

Materials

Water

Plastic wrap

Two small peanut-butter jars

Large jar

Soft, thick cloth string (non-wax covering), 20 inches

Epsom salt

Towel or washcloth

Two small washers

Procedure

Fill the large jar almost three-fourths full of water. Slowly add the Epsom salt, stirring continuously until no more salt will dissolve. Pour the solution into two small peanut-butter jars. Tie the washers to the ends of the string. Place the towel (washcloth) on a sheet of plastic wrap in an area where it won't be moved for several days. Place the jars on top of the cloth. Dip the entire string in one jar and remove. Place one end of the string in each jar and form a loop between jars and over the cloth. The string should sag about halfway down between the jars. Do NOT touch or move the materials. Check once a day, for six days, to see what forms on the string and on the cloth. The cave structures that hang down from the string are called stalactites, and the deposits on the cloth are called stalagmites.

Observations

Which formed first, the stalactites or the stalagmites? Were the stalactites or the stalagmites larger? How does the color of the jars' liquid compare with the color of the stalactites and the stalagmites?

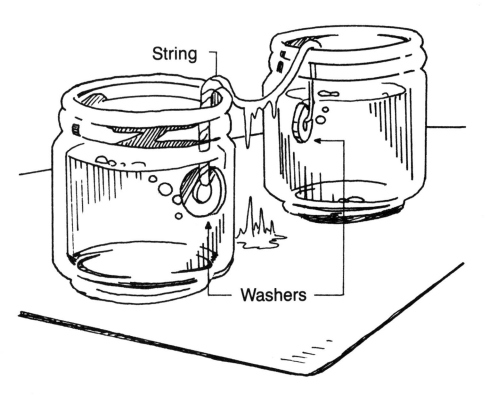

String

Washers

Discussion

This activity is a model of how cave structures form. The water with dissolved Epsom salt soaks the string and slowly drips from the low point. The Epsom salt cannot be seen moving from the cups, but it appears when the water evaporates.

In a cave, water with dissolved minerals (such as the Epsom salt in this experiment) drips from the ceiling of the cave to the floor. As the water evaporates, minerals are left behind both at the ceiling and the floor. These deposits slowly develop into stone icicles. Frequently, stalactites and stalagmites take 500 years to grow one inch. An easy way to remember which is which is that stalactites are spelled with a "c" and hang from the ceiling while stalagmites are spelled with a "g" and form on the ground. When you visit a real cave, never touch a stalactite or stalagmite because the oil on your hand will stop the movement of the dissolved minerals. The stalactites and stalagmites will then never grow larger.

Other things to try

Substitute brown sugar for the Epsom salt. Compare these deposits with Epsom salt deposits.

HOW CAN WE CLEAN UP DIRTY WATER?

30

Materials

Two peanut-butter jars   Measuring cup
Tablespoon   Water
Purple grape juice
Activated charcoal (available at aquarium/pet shops)

Procedure

Fill a measuring cup with about 3/4 cup (about 180 ml) of water. Add slightly more than 1/4 cup (about 60 ml) of grape juice to the water. Stir until the color is well mixed. Put almost 1/2 cup (about 120 ml) of the weak grape juice into each jar. Add two tablespoons of activated charcoal to one jar. Tighten the lids on each jar. Place the jars in a place where they won't need to be moved for at least five days. Each day check the color of the weak grape juice in each jar.

Dump the contents of the jars in a place outside recommended by an adult.

Observations

What happens to the color of the weak grape juice in each jar? Which day had the biggest change in color in the jar with charcoal?

Discussion

The jar with the activated charcoal should get lighter each day. The grape juice appears to be leaving the water because the grape coloring settles in the small openings of the activated charcoal. However, the jar with no charcoal will be about the same color. This experiment simulates the dirty water left after we have finished using water in our homes.

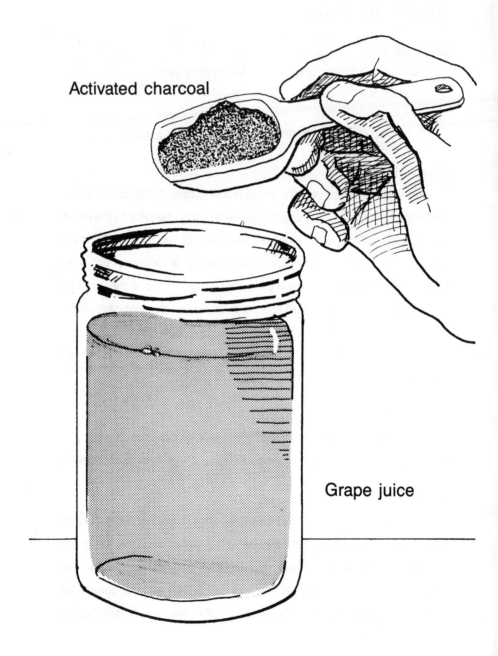

Activated charcoal

Grape juice

The dirty water that leaves our homes goes to sewage treatment plants. Without the treatment, our rivers and streams would be very much more polluted (dirty). Activated charcoal is not the same as the charcoal we use in our grills and barbecues. The activated charcoal is specially treated with steam, which gets in the tiny cracks. Activated charcoal is used in sewage treatment to clean the water. If you have an aquarium, you use it to keep the water clean.

If the water wasn't cleaned, it would pollute the soil it touches. It would also be harmful to fish and plants that live in the water. Nobody would want to drink these polluted waters. Therefore, we need to clean up water before it is put back into the rivers.

Other things to try

Repeat the experiment, using six drops of food coloring rather than the grape juice. Does it take longer to clean up the colored water?

Repeat the experiment to determine how temperature affects the results. Compare equal containers where one was placed inside the refrigerator and the other kept at room temperature.

Repeat the experiment, using less charcoal. Does the amount of charcoal change the amount of weak grape juice that can be cleaned up?

Where to Get Science Supplies

The following companies sell mineral samples, streak plates, and other science supplies. To order materials for your experiments, write or telephone the nearest company to find out about prices. Then send your order to the company with a check or money order to cover the cost. You can also ask your teacher to order materials for you on school stationary.

Carolina Biological Supply
   2700 York Road
   Burlington, NC 27215
   (919) 584-0381

Edmund Scientific Company
   101 East Glouchester Pike
   Barrington, NJ 08007-1380
   (609) 573-6250

Fisher Scientific
   4901 W. Le Moyne Street
   Chicago, IL 60651
   (800) 621-4769

Frey Scientific Company
   905 Hickory Lane
   P.O. Box 8101
   Mansfield, OH 44905
   (800) 225-FREY

Sargent-Welch
   7400 North Linder Avenue
   P.O. Box 1026
   Skokie, IL 60077
   (800) 727-4368

Science Kit and Boreal
   Laboratories
   777 East Park Drive
   Tonawanda, NY 14150-6782
   (800) 828-7777

—OR—

Science Kit and Boreal
   Laboratories
   P.O. Box 2726
   Sante Fe Springs, CA 90670-4490

Ward's Natural Science
   Establishment, Inc.
   5100 West Henrietta Road
   P.O. Box 92912
   Rochester, NY 14692
   (800) 962-2660

COMPLETE LIST OF MATERIALS
USED IN EXPERIMENTS

Activated charcoal
adding machine tape
apple juice

Baking soda
balloon
bleach
board
bucket

Chalk
charcoal briquets
 or bricks
chart paper
coffee filter
cranberry juice
cups (plastic)

Distilled water
drinking glass

Epsom salt

Grape juice (purple)
grass seed or transplanted
 grass
gravel (aquarium or small
 driveway)

Hammer (small)
hand lens or magnifying
 glass

Jars with lids
juice cans

Knife

Lemon juice
lemonade mix
lime (powdered)
liquid detergent

Magnet (ceramic)

masking tape
Mason jar (pint)
measuring cup
measuring spoons
medicine dropper
metric ruler
milk cartons (quart and
 half-gallon)
milk jugs (plastic)
milk of magnesia
mineral samples, such as:
 calcite, galena, gypsum,
 halite, hematite, magnetite,
 pyrite, quartz, talc, etc.
modeling clay

Nail file
nails (steel)
navy beans
newspaper

Orange juice

Pans
panty hose
paper
paper towels
peanut butter jars with lids
pen (red)
pencils
pennies
pH paper and color chart
pie pan
pill bottle (plastic)
pitcher
plaster of Paris
plastic bag (self-sealing)
plastic wrap
plate (glass)
protractor

Radish seeds
razor blade (single-edged)
refrigerator freezer

rock salt
rubber bands
ruler

Sandbox or beach
 sand
sandpaper (fine and
 coarse)
saucepan
saucer
shoebox
soil (such as potting,
 sand, or garden)
soft drinks
soda bottle (plastic)
spade and/or trowel
sprinkler can
stapler
string

Table knife
tablespoon
teaspoon
tile (unglazed
 porcelain)
 or streak plate
tomato juice
towel
tweezers

Vinegar (white)

Washcloth
washers
watch with second
 hand
water
wax paper
window cleaner
wood blocks or bricks

INDEX